3·6·9 Manifestation Journal for Beginners

3·6·9

MANIFESTATION JOURNAL

FOR BEGINNERS

A 12-Week Journal for Achieving Your Goals

LINDSAY ROSE

ROCKRIDGE
PRESS

This journal belongs to:

_____

Introduction

Welcome to the greatest journey you will ever take—the journey within yourself! I'm Lindsay Rose, manifestation and mindset coach, and I'm thrilled that you're here, ready and willing to create a life that you love. I discovered manifestation six years ago when I was desperately trying to make my life better. I was intrigued by the idea that we have the ability to create our own reality. Over the course of the last six years, I've read countless books and studied many methods on how to actually manifest, and I decided to pursue a career teaching others to do the same. My success and the impact I've been able to make on the lives of others are all due to the concepts I'll be sharing in this book.

Somewhere during my pursuit of knowledge around the idea of reality creation, I was led to the work of Nikola Tesla (more on him later) and the 369 manifestation method. I began applying the method to my own manifestation journey, and the results were incredible. I was attracting amazing things into my life as if it were magic.

I now teach thousands of people all over the world to create their own amazing and magical lives using the 369 method. My clients have manifested pregnancies, unexpected money, promotions, romantic partners, weight loss, and so much more using the process that I outline in this book.

All change begins with an awareness that things *can* be different for you. May you keep an open heart and mind as you explore the ideas that follow. Allow yourself to trust in the process and know that you were led right here, right now for a reason. I can't wait for you to see the magic of manifestation unfold in your life. Have fun!

How to Use This Journal

The purpose of this journal is to increase your manifestation potential through the process of deliberate creation and self-awareness. This journal was designed to help you find clarity about what you would like to experience in your life and begin to reprogram your subconscious mind to assist you with aligning energetically with that desire.

Part One of this journal provides an overview of the 369 method, how it works, and how you can use this journal to practice it. Along with some examples, the prompts in this section will help prepare you to begin your own manifestation journey. Then, in Part Two, you may begin by writing your own manifestations in the daily tracking pages. Using the lines provided in these pages, you will write down your manifestation daily—three times in the morning, six times in the afternoon, and nine times in the evening. This may get repetitive, but that's the idea. When we write or speak something consistently and with repetition, it will eventually become automatic. I recommend starting with one specific manifestation at a time until it comes into physical form. You can certainly add other manifestations as you go along that will ultimately lead to your main desires.

After you write your manifestations down, you will be invited to visualize yourself accomplishing your goal or already having the outcome you're asking for. Weekly and monthly check-in pages will prompt you to dive deeper into the feeling of having your desire via journal prompts, practices, and exercises. While this journal leaves room for twelve weeks' worth of manifestations, in the beginning it's important that you stick with this process for at least twenty-one days in order to create new patterns of thought and feeling in the subconscious mind. Resources are included at the end of this journal to help you learn more about manifesting and reality creation.

PART
I

AN INTRODUCTION TO THE 3·6·9 MANIFESTATION METHOD

What Is the 369 Method?

The 369 method is a powerful, math-based manifestation practice that was derived from inventor Nikola Tesla. He is known for having said, "If you want to find the secrets of the universe, think in terms of energy, frequency, and vibration."

When it comes to manifesting, the numbers three, six, and nine are considered to be the "divine code" of the universe. The number three is a direct link to the universe, six is our inner strength, and nine helps us release negativity. We incorporate this 369 sequence in writing manifestations, in essence, to create unity with the universe.

Put simply, math is a universal language that wasn't created—it was discovered. To demonstrate the uniqueness of these numbers (3, 6, and 9), let's refer to the binary system. If you take the number 1 and double it, you get 2. Double number 2 and you get 4 . . . and so the pattern would resemble this: 1, 2, 4, 8, 16, 32, etc.

You'll notice that the numbers 3, 6, and 9 never appear in this pattern. This intrigued Nikola Tesla so much so that he devoted his life to these mysterious numbers.

How the 369 Method Works

According to the Law of Vibration, everything in the universe is in motion. That means that you are essentially a field of vibrating energy that emits a specific frequency based on your emotional state. To help you better understand the concept of frequencies, think of your every thought as a vibration. If you give that thought your attention for long enough, it is then translated into an emotion, which creates your energetic state of being. Therefore, what you think and how you feel determine your personal frequency. The Law of Attraction states that like attracts like, meaning that your frequency acts like a magnetic field that attracts experiences, people, and things that match your energy.

The 369 method works with the subconscious mind, using consistent, repetitive affirmations or manifestations to help you energetically align with what you desire. The process is simple. You write what you want to manifest *as if it has already manifested* three times in the morning, six times in the afternoon, and nine times in the evening. In doing so, you are creating a strong intention, elevated emotional state, and focused mind, which places you on the frequency necessary to attract your manifestation.

The 369 method also functions as a tool to help shift negative thoughts into more optimistic ways of thinking. What you consistently repeat to yourself becomes your belief system. Your belief systems are the primary source of how you see the world and ultimately determine what you are an energetic match for.

Writing Your Manifestations

Believe it or not, most of us are living life unintentionally, meaning we don't actually take the time to be intentional about where we'd like to go or what we would ideally like to experience. I call this living by default. When we don't choose the destinations, life chooses for us based on our default subconscious programs. What do you truly want? The universe needs to know what to deliver, and your subconscious mind needs to understand where it has to guide you.

Setting intentions is the beginning of the manifestation process, and it allows you to be purposeful about your life. It gives you the creative control to decide where to place your target. This allows you to more specifically direct your energy. As life coach and motivational speaker Tony Robbins says, "Where focus goes, energy flows."

When writing your manifestations in this journal, you should write as if your desire has already manifested. A few things to keep in mind:

1. Begin with how you feel about what you have manifested, for example, "I am so happy and grateful now that . . ."

2. Write in present or past tense. Use words like "I am" or "I have." Stay away from "I want" or any future tense.

3. Include words that are descriptive and inclusive of the five senses ("I see," "I touch," "I hear," and "I feel").

Here are a few sample manifestations, using the format laid out above, to give you a clearer sense of how to write your own:

"I am so grateful for the love and support that I feel from my friends and family."

"I am so excited to have received this promotion at a job that I am passionate about."

"I feel so appreciative of the time I spend traveling and seeing new sights."

Uncovering Your Deepest Desires

Most of us can describe in detail the things that we *do not* want to experience, but we never really take the time to define the things that we *do* want. There is immense value in knowing what you don't want because it points you clearly in the direction of desire. Unwanted experiences create opportunity for us to choose what we prefer.

To help guide you toward uncovering what you truly desire, spend some time asking yourself the following questions:

What is something I'm currently experiencing that I *do not* want to experience?

Example: I am so over being anxious about money.

_____

_____

_____

How does it feel to be in this position?

Example: I feel like I'm powerless.

_____

_____

_____

What would you like to be experiencing instead?

Example: I would love to be financially secure and live abundantly.

_____

_____

_____

How do you want to feel?

Example: I desire to feel empowered and free.

_____

_____

_____

So, in the example, your desire would be: I desire to be more financially secure so that I can live abundantly and feel empowered and free.

EMBODIMENT PRACTICE

Once you have a more clearly defined desire in mind, you can use this practice to tap into the energy of that desire:

Close your eyes and begin by relaxing each and every muscle in your body, starting from the top of your head down to your toes.

Next, bring forward, into your mind's eye, an image of your desired manifestation.

What is a visual representation of the intended desire? How would you know this desire has manifested for you? Create the scene in your mind like a movie.

Allow yourself to be fully immersed in the experience, taking in all the colors, sounds, smells, and textures.

See yourself in this reality as if it's happening *now* through your eyes.

What does it look and feel like to have your desired outcome?

Beginning Your Manifestation Journey

Now that you have a clear understanding of how the 369 method works and why it's so powerful, it's time to get started on your manifestation journey. The key to success during this process is consistency. Repetition is the key to creating change at the subconscious level, which is where 95 percent of our reality is created.

Once the belief changes, you will begin to notice subtle shifts in your response to your reality. As you change internally, your outside world will reflect back to you who you are being. Manifestation is an internal process. What you think and feel on the inside is ultimately what you will experience as a reflection in your reality. It's akin to looking in the mirror. You wouldn't expect your reflection to smile first. It has to start with you.

It is important not only to believe in the affirmations you're creating and repeating, but also to believe and trust in the manifestation process as a whole. Keep in mind that it takes time for your reality to catch up with your new frequency or energy field. Place your trust in the unseen and have patience with the process.

PART
II

YOUR
12-WEEK
3·6·9
MANIFESTATION
JOURNAL

 **Date**＿＿＿＿＿

MORNING PRACTICE

_____

_____

_____

AFTERNOON PRACTICE

_____

_____

_____

_____

_____

_____

EVENING PRACTICE

_____

_____

_____

_____

_____

_____

_____

_____

_____

DAY 2 Date_____

MORNING PRACTICE

_____
_____
_____

AFTERNOON PRACTICE

_____
_____
_____
_____
_____
_____

EVENING PRACTICE

_____
_____
_____
_____
_____
_____
_____
_____
_____

DAY 3 Date_____

MORNING PRACTICE

_____

_____

_____

AFTERNOON PRACTICE

_____

_____

_____

_____

_____

_____

EVENING PRACTICE

_____

_____

_____

_____

_____

_____

_____

_____

_____

DAY 4   Date_____

MORNING PRACTICE

_____

_____

_____

AFTERNOON PRACTICE

_____

_____

_____

_____

_____

_____

EVENING PRACTICE

_____

_____

_____

_____

_____

_____

_____

_____

DAY 5 Date_____

MORNING PRACTICE

_____

_____

_____

AFTERNOON PRACTICE

_____

_____

_____

_____

_____

_____

EVENING PRACTICE

_____

_____

_____

_____

_____

_____

_____

_____

DAY 6 Date_____

MORNING PRACTICE

_____
_____
_____

AFTERNOON PRACTICE

_____
_____
_____
_____
_____
_____

EVENING PRACTICE

_____
_____
_____
_____
_____
_____
_____
_____
_____

 **Date**_____

MORNING PRACTICE

_____

_____

_____

AFTERNOON PRACTICE

_____

_____

_____

_____

_____

_____

EVENING PRACTICE

_____

_____

_____

_____

_____

_____

_____

_____

_____

WEEKLY CHECK-IN

*"Ask for what you want and be
prepared to get it."*
—MAYA ANGELOU

How are you feeling so far? Have you noticed any shifts?

_____

_____

_____

_____

_____

CELEBRATING MICRO-MANIFESTATIONS

It's important to notice subtle shifts and micro-manifestations as you begin this journey. This helps build trust in the process. Take a moment to reflect on the week and notice the micro-transformations that are already happening. It may just be that you felt calmer or that you responded differently to circumstances that would have otherwise triggered you. As you start to become aware of the little aha moments, you activate your ability to tap into even more magic. As a practice, I invite you to start with the simple phrase "I'm already doing it" or "It's already happening" each time you experience a win. In the acknowledgment of micro-wins, you are sending the message to the universe that you're noticing and therefore ready to receive even more.

Choosing to See the Shifts

Take a few moments to list everything amazing that happened this week, even if it was a tiny victory. This can look like:

1. Remaining calm in a difficult situation

2. Noticing more beauty around you

3. Having a difficult conversation

4. Experiencing a micro-manifestation (evidence you're moving in the right direction)

WHAT ARE YOUR WINS FOR THIS WEEK?

_____

_____

_____

_____

_____

_____

What are you going to do to celebrate these little victories? Maybe it's a happy dance, a special dinner, or a bouquet of flowers. Find a way to give yourself credit for even the little wins.

_____

_____

_____

_____

_____

DAY 8 Date_____

MORNING PRACTICE

_____

_____

_____

AFTERNOON PRACTICE

_____

_____

_____

_____

_____

_____

EVENING PRACTICE

_____

_____

_____

_____

_____

_____

_____

_____

 **DAY 9** Date_____

MORNING PRACTICE

_____

_____

_____

AFTERNOON PRACTICE

_____

_____

_____

_____

_____

_____

EVENING PRACTICE

_____

_____

_____

_____

_____

_____

_____

_____

_____

DAY 10 Date_____

MORNING PRACTICE

_____

_____

_____

AFTERNOON PRACTICE

_____

_____

_____

_____

_____

_____

EVENING PRACTICE

_____

_____

_____

_____

_____

_____

_____

_____

DAY 11 Date_____

MORNING PRACTICE

_____

_____

_____

AFTERNOON PRACTICE

_____

_____

_____

_____

_____

_____

EVENING PRACTICE

_____

_____

_____

_____

_____

_____

_____

_____

_____

DAY 12 Date_____

MORNING PRACTICE

_____

_____

_____

AFTERNOON PRACTICE

_____

_____

_____

_____

_____

_____

EVENING PRACTICE

_____

_____

_____

_____

_____

_____

_____

_____

_____

DAY 13

Date_____

MORNING PRACTICE

_____
_____
_____

AFTERNOON PRACTICE

_____
_____
_____
_____
_____
_____

EVENING PRACTICE

_____
_____
_____
_____
_____
_____
_____
_____
_____

DAY 14   Date_____

MORNING PRACTICE

_____

_____

_____

AFTERNOON PRACTICE

_____

_____

_____

_____

_____

_____

EVENING PRACTICE

_____

_____

_____

_____

_____

_____

_____

_____

WEEKLY CHECK-IN

"Once you make a decision, the universe conspires to make it happen."

—RALPH WALDO EMERSON

How are you feeling this week? What changes have you noticed?

_____

_____

_____

_____

_____

_____

USING YOUR IMAGINATION

The most valuable tool we have as humans is our imagination. Our imagination is what allows us to envision our dreams before they come to fruition. Being able to see our manifestation in our mind is key to being able to experience it in our life. This is how we create new neural pathways in the brain and ultimately how we access the feeling of it before it arrives.

Close your eyes, take a deep breath in, and bring your attention inward. Allow yourself to bring forward the vision in your mind of your ideal day. Imagine that you are waking up in the morning and, as you open your eyes, you are right where you desire to be.

Your Ideal Day

What is the first thing you see when you open your eyes?

_____

_____

_____

Who are you with?

_____

_____

_____

What do you have planned for the day?

_____

_____

_____

Where are you going?

_____

_____

_____

Take note of anything that stands out to you. Practice playing this mental scene in your mind as you move into next week. I recommend playing this mental movie throughout your day, especially when your mind drifts to negativity. This will help you remain focused on your vision and will assist your brain in helping make it a reality for you.

DAY 15   Date_____

MORNING PRACTICE

_____

_____

_____

AFTERNOON PRACTICE

_____

_____

_____

_____

_____

_____

EVENING PRACTICE

_____

_____

_____

_____

_____

_____

_____

_____

_____

DAY 16 Date_____

MORNING PRACTICE

_____

_____

_____

AFTERNOON PRACTICE

_____

_____

_____

_____

_____

_____

EVENING PRACTICE

_____

_____

_____

_____

_____

_____

_____

_____

 **DAY 17** Date_____

MORNING PRACTICE

_____
_____
_____
_____

AFTERNOON PRACTICE

_____
_____
_____
_____
_____
_____
_____

EVENING PRACTICE

_____
_____
_____
_____
_____
_____
_____
_____
_____
_____

DAY 18 Date_____

MORNING PRACTICE

_____
_____
_____

AFTERNOON PRACTICE

_____
_____
_____
_____
_____
_____

EVENING PRACTICE

_____
_____
_____
_____
_____
_____
_____
_____
_____

DAY 19   Date_____

MORNING PRACTICE

_____

_____

_____

AFTERNOON PRACTICE

_____

_____

_____

_____

_____

EVENING PRACTICE

_____

_____

_____

_____

_____

_____

_____

_____

DAY 20 Date_____

MORNING PRACTICE

_____

_____

_____

AFTERNOON PRACTICE

_____

_____

_____

_____

_____

_____

EVENING PRACTICE

_____

_____

_____

_____

_____

_____

_____

_____

DAY 21 Date_____

MORNING PRACTICE

_____

_____

_____

AFTERNOON PRACTICE

_____

_____

_____

_____

_____

_____

EVENING PRACTICE

_____

_____

_____

_____

_____

_____

_____

_____

WEEKLY CHECK-IN

*"Keep your mind fixed on what you want in life:
not on what you don't want."*
—NAPOLEON HILL

How are you feeling this week? What has been the biggest realization so far?

_____

_____

_____

OVERCOMING BLOCKS

It's common to feel even more resistance in your life as you stretch to match a new frequency. You may notice that fears, doubts, and uncertainty creep in. It's a very normal part of the process. This happens as your mindset changes because your brain can't predict how it will happen or if you even deserve to have it. Therefore, it will try to keep you from moving forward.

You can easily identify where these beliefs are blocking you with this simple practice:

Step 1: State your affirmation out loud.

Step 2: Say it with confidence.

Step 3: Notice what thoughts pop into your head that say it's not possible or probable. These are limiting beliefs/thoughts that are counter to what you desire (basically an energetic standstill).

Belief Buster

Choose a limiting belief to work through:

_____

1. Where did you pick up this belief? See if you can recall the first
    time you started to believe this. It's okay if you can't identify
    the origin—it just helps if you understand where you picked up
    the belief.

    _____

    _____

    _____

2. Is this belief true? Most of our belief systems aren't based in
    truth; they have just been passed down to us. Take a moment
    to discredit or disprove this belief.

    _____

    _____

    _____

3. What would you prefer to believe instead? Treat this new belief
    as an affirmation to begin the process of reprogramming it into
    your subconscious. Remember, repetition is key.

    _____

    _____

    _____

Expert tip: Write your new belief on a sticky note and place it where
you will see it every day. This will help get it into your subconscious.

DAY 22 Date_____

MORNING PRACTICE

_____

_____

_____

AFTERNOON PRACTICE

_____

_____

_____

_____

_____

_____

EVENING PRACTICE

_____

_____

_____

_____

_____

_____

_____

_____

DAY 23

Date_____

MORNING PRACTICE

AFTERNOON PRACTICE

EVENING PRACTICE

DAY 24

Date_____

MORNING PRACTICE

_____

_____

_____

AFTERNOON PRACTICE

_____

_____

_____

_____

_____

_____

EVENING PRACTICE

_____

_____

_____

_____

_____

_____

_____

_____

DAY 25

Date_____

MORNING PRACTICE

_____

_____

_____

AFTERNOON PRACTICE

_____

_____

_____

_____

_____

_____

EVENING PRACTICE

_____

_____

_____

_____

_____

_____

_____

_____

_____

DAY 26   Date_____

MORNING PRACTICE

_____
_____
_____

AFTERNOON PRACTICE

_____
_____
_____
_____
_____

EVENING PRACTICE

_____
_____
_____
_____
_____
_____
_____
_____

DAY 27 Date_____

MORNING PRACTICE

_____

_____

_____

AFTERNOON PRACTICE

_____

_____

_____

_____

_____

_____

EVENING PRACTICE

_____

_____

_____

_____

_____

_____

_____

_____

_____

DAY 28   Date_____

MORNING PRACTICE

_____
_____
_____

AFTERNOON PRACTICE

_____
_____
_____
_____
_____
_____

EVENING PRACTICE

_____
_____
_____
_____
_____
_____
_____
_____
_____

WEEKLY CHECK-IN

*"Ask once, believe you have received, and all
you have to do to receive is feel good."*
—RHONDA BYRNE

How are you feeling this week? What has been the biggest realization so far?

_____

_____

_____

_____

_____

_____

_____

I'LL TAKE SOME OF THAT!

One of my favorite practices is to consciously acknowledge the things in your environment or reality as if you're choosing from a catalog of what you would like to create. Most of the time when we see someone or something that we would like to be or have, our initial response is jealousy or envy. To flip the script, whenever you see something you'd like to have, claim it! State to yourself or out loud, "I'll take some of that," or "Yes, more of that." Not only does this help you snap out of lack consciousness, but it allows you to more consciously choose what you'd like to include in your experience.

What You Judge in Others Is Also in You

Typically, when we feel a sense of judgment or jealousy toward something someone has, it's because we don't believe fully in our own ability to have that. Jealousy and envy are the ultimate blocks to being able to attract your desires because they send the message that the thing you want is "bad."

To help you better understand where you may be unconsciously blocking yourself, ask yourself:

What do I typically judge in others?

_____

_____

_____

Is this quality or trait something I also contain or reject about myself?

_____

_____

_____

What are the things I get most jealous of when others accomplish or attract them?

_____

_____

_____

When you start to notice yourself judging or feeling jealous this week, choose to celebrate the victories or success. In the celebration of others, you magnetize more into your life.

MONTHLY CHECK-IN

*"The main event has never been the manifestation;
the main event has always been the way you
feel moment by moment."*
—ESTHER AND JERRY HICKS

What have been the biggest shifts for you over the last month?

_____

_____

_____

Do you have any fears or doubts arising? If so, what are they?

_____

_____

_____

WHEN IT FEELS LIKE IT'S NOT HAPPENING

As you move through this manifestation journey, it's easy to
get discouraged when you don't see things changing as quickly
as you'd like them to. The mind has a tendency to notice the
absence of the things we desire and therefore puts us into a
state of not having it or of lack. Lack consciousness is the block
to all manifestations. What you focus on will expand, so it's
important to choose to focus on what *is* working.

Notice if you are still giving your energy to the areas of lack
in your life. Do you tend to focus on where your manifestation is
or why it's not happening?

Gratitude Is the Attitude of Abundance

This exercise is designed to help you shift from a mentality of lack to noticing all the abundance and magic that surround you in this moment.

WHAT AM I GRATEFUL FOR?	WHY?
1.	
2.	
3.	
4.	
5.	
6.	
7.	
8.	
9.	
10.	

When you take time to notice all the blessings you have in your life, it helps place you in a vibration to receive even more of what you desire. Gratitude and appreciation are magnetic forces that bring forth even more to be grateful for. Take this practice with you throughout the month and begin to notice all the wonderful things you already have in your life.

DAY 29 Date_____

MORNING PRACTICE

_____

_____

_____

AFTERNOON PRACTICE

_____

_____

_____

_____

_____

_____

EVENING PRACTICE

_____

_____

_____

_____

_____

_____

_____

_____

_____

DAY 30

Date_____

MORNING PRACTICE

_____
_____
_____

AFTERNOON PRACTICE

_____
_____
_____
_____
_____
_____

EVENING PRACTICE

_____
_____
_____
_____
_____
_____
_____
_____
_____

DAY 31

Date_____

MORNING PRACTICE

_____

_____

_____

AFTERNOON PRACTICE

_____

_____

_____

_____

_____

_____

EVENING PRACTICE

_____

_____

_____

_____

_____

_____

_____

_____

DAY 32 Date_____

MORNING PRACTICE

_____

_____

_____

AFTERNOON PRACTICE

_____

_____

_____

_____

_____

_____

EVENING PRACTICE

_____

_____

_____

_____

_____

_____

_____

_____

DAY 33   Date_____

MORNING PRACTICE

_____
_____
_____

AFTERNOON PRACTICE

_____
_____
_____
_____
_____
_____

EVENING PRACTICE

_____
_____
_____
_____
_____
_____
_____
_____

DAY 34 Date_____

MORNING PRACTICE

_____

_____

_____

AFTERNOON PRACTICE

_____

_____

_____

_____

_____

_____

EVENING PRACTICE

_____

_____

_____

_____

_____

_____

_____

_____

_____

DAY 35　Date_____

MORNING PRACTICE

_____

_____

_____

AFTERNOON PRACTICE

_____

_____

_____

_____

_____

_____

EVENING PRACTICE

_____

_____

_____

_____

_____

_____

_____

_____

WEEKLY CHECK-IN

*"Whatever is going on in your mind,
you are attracting to you."*

—BOB PROCTOR

What changes have you noticed this week? Are you finding it easier
to catch your negative thoughts?

_____

_____

_____

_____

_____

BECOMING THE GATEKEEPER

It is only through awareness that we can create change. What
we are unaware of has unconscious control over our reality.
Being aware of what you are thinking throughout the day is the
key to being able to become a more intentional and conscious
creator. You ultimately have to become the gatekeeper of your
mind. We tend to drift into negative thoughts or worry when
we aren't intentional with our thoughts. This usually happens
when we are in the mundane moments of our day. When you
are taking a shower, brushing your teeth, driving to work, or
just doing your day-to-day tasks this week, practice using
these moments to choose your point of focus. Spend a few
moments directing your thoughts and mental images toward
your manifestation.

From Worry to Wonder

What areas of your life do you tend to worry about the most?

_____

_____

_____

What is the "what if" that you attached to this worry? For example, "What if I never find my soul mate?"

_____

_____

_____

What if something amazing happens instead? Choose a positive "what if" statement to practice.

_____

_____

_____

What are some other paths that you can't see at the moment? For example, if you're worrying about money, perhaps you might receive an unexpected refund or win a lottery.

_____

_____

_____

When we flip the script, it allows us to expand our mind into the positive and potential of something we would prefer to experience.

DAY 36

Date_____

MORNING PRACTICE

_____

_____

_____

AFTERNOON PRACTICE

_____

_____

_____

_____

_____

_____

EVENING PRACTICE

_____

_____

_____

_____

_____

_____

_____

_____

_____

DAY 37   Date_____

MORNING PRACTICE

_____

_____

_____

AFTERNOON PRACTICE

_____

_____

_____

_____

_____

_____

EVENING PRACTICE

_____

_____

_____

_____

_____

_____

_____

_____

_____

DAY 38   Date_____

MORNING PRACTICE

_____

_____

_____

AFTERNOON PRACTICE

_____

_____

_____

_____

_____

_____

EVENING PRACTICE

_____

_____

_____

_____

_____

_____

_____

_____

DAY 39   Date_____

MORNING PRACTICE

_____

_____

_____

AFTERNOON PRACTICE

_____

_____

_____

_____

_____

EVENING PRACTICE

_____

_____

_____

_____

_____

_____

_____

_____

DAY 40　Date_____

MORNING PRACTICE

_____

_____

_____

AFTERNOON PRACTICE

_____

_____

_____

_____

_____

_____

EVENING PRACTICE

_____

_____

_____

_____

_____

_____

_____

_____

DAY 41   Date_____

MORNING PRACTICE

_____
_____
_____

AFTERNOON PRACTICE

_____
_____
_____
_____
_____
_____

EVENING PRACTICE

_____
_____
_____
_____
_____
_____
_____
_____
_____

DAY 42

Date_____

MORNING PRACTICE

_____

_____

_____

AFTERNOON PRACTICE

_____

_____

_____

_____

_____

_____

EVENING PRACTICE

_____

_____

_____

_____

_____

_____

_____

_____

WEEKLY CHECK-IN

"The Universe is not outside of you. Look inside yourself; everything that you want, you already are."

—RUMI

What changes have you noticed this week? How do you feel overall?

_____

_____

_____

_____

_____

_____

WINKS FROM THE UNIVERSE

Seeing signs and synchronicities is like a wink from the universe that you're on the right path and your manifestation is getting closer. We are constantly cocreating our reality with our higher self or our higher mind. This aspect of you has a higher vantage point and is able to see clearly the path that will lead you to your desire. The higher self will often show us repeating numbers or even animals as symbols to let us know that we are not alone in the process.

Asking for a sign is also helpful when you aren't quite sure of which decision to make or which way to go on your path. This helps strengthen your relationship with the universe and your higher self.

Step 1: Choose a sign or symbol that you would like to be shown. Just choose the first thing that comes to mind.

Step 2: Close your eyes and send your request: "Dear universe, please show me a _____ as confirmation that I'm on the right path or that I should make the decisions to _____."

Step 3: Let it go and be patient.

Step 4: When you notice the sign, send gratitude to acknowledge that you have received the sign, and take appropriate action.

Expert tip: Remember, not receiving the sign is actually a sign. If you need to make a decision within a certain time frame, be sure to include that in your request.

How to Find Clarity When Making Decisions

Have you ever found yourself caught between multiple decisions, unsure of the right path to take? Here's the secret: There is no "right path." No matter what choice you make, it will always lead you where you need to be for your highest good. However, some paths do bring with them lessons for us to learn rather than the blessings we're calling for. This exercise is a great tool to help you determine which path or time line would have the least resistance.

List all the pros and cons of each option or decision you have to make and then compare and evaluate. As simple as this may seem, sometimes we just need to take a moment to be honest with ourselves about what we have to lose and gain from our decision. This exercise alone can bring greater clarity.

CONTINUED ON NEXT PAGE

OPTION 1	OPTION 2
WHAT WILL I GAIN FROM MAKING THIS DECISION?	**WHAT WILL I GAIN FROM MAKING THIS DECISION?**
WHAT WILL I LOSE BY MAKING THIS DECISION?	**WHAT WILL I LOSE BY MAKING THIS DECISION?**

DAY 43   Date_____

MORNING PRACTICE

_____
_____
_____

AFTERNOON PRACTICE

_____
_____
_____
_____
_____

EVENING PRACTICE

_____
_____
_____
_____
_____
_____
_____
_____

DAY 44　Date_____

MORNING PRACTICE

_____

_____

_____

AFTERNOON PRACTICE

_____

_____

_____

_____

_____

_____

EVENING PRACTICE

_____

_____

_____

_____

_____

_____

_____

_____

DAY 45 Date_____

MORNING PRACTICE

_____
_____
_____

AFTERNOON PRACTICE

_____
_____
_____
_____
_____
_____

EVENING PRACTICE

_____
_____
_____
_____
_____
_____
_____
_____

DAY 46 Date_____

MORNING PRACTICE

_____

_____

_____

AFTERNOON PRACTICE

_____

_____

_____

_____

_____

_____

EVENING PRACTICE

_____

_____

_____

_____

_____

_____

_____

_____

DAY 47   Date_____

MORNING PRACTICE

_____

_____

_____

AFTERNOON PRACTICE

_____

_____

_____

_____

_____

_____

EVENING PRACTICE

_____

_____

_____

_____

_____

_____

_____

_____

DAY 48

Date_____

MORNING PRACTICE

_____

_____

_____

AFTERNOON PRACTICE

_____

_____

_____

_____

_____

_____

EVENING PRACTICE

_____

_____

_____

_____

_____

_____

_____

_____

_____

DAY 49

Date_____

MORNING PRACTICE

_____

_____

_____

AFTERNOON PRACTICE

_____

_____

_____

_____

_____

_____

EVENING PRACTICE

_____

_____

_____

_____

_____

_____

_____

_____

WEEKLY CHECK-IN

"We become what we think about."
—EARL NIGHTINGALE

What has been the biggest realization this week? What is one thing you're proud of yourself for this week?

_____

_____

_____

_____

_____

_____

WHAT GOES IN, MUST COME OUT

Our minds are designed to look for possible risks or upcoming trouble, especially given the society that we live in. We are inundated with fear through the media and social channels, and it's fairly easy to get swept up in it all. What we allow to come into our mind is ultimately what will come out. As a practice this week, pay attention to what you are consuming—whether it be television programming, podcasts, books, or even conversations you're engaging in. If it doesn't leave you feeling lighter, inspired, or lifted, it may be a good time to consider limiting your exposure. Keep in mind that the subconscious is very impressionable as you are falling asleep at night. Be mindful of what you are watching or listening to right as you're drifting off to sleep.

What You Focus on Expands

Being able to focus is a skill or a muscle that must be flexed and strengthened. We live in a society that encourages instant gratification, which lessens our ability to focus for longer periods of time. This exercise is designed to help you train your focus, which speeds up your manifestation.

Step 1: Begin by bringing to mind an idea of something small. For example:

- Butterflies
- An apple
- Roses
- A random sequence of numbers

The item I choose to focus on is _____.

Step 2: Bring your chosen item into focus in your mind. See it vividly. Imagine touching it, smelling it, hearing it (if applicable). The idea is to create strong imagery to impress upon the subconscious.

Step 3: (optional) Place a photo of this image somewhere you will see it every day this week.

Step 4: Take note of every time you see this item during the week. It can appear in many different forms and places. For instance, if you chose a blue butterfly, it could show up on a billboard, an emoji from a friend, or even a tattoo on someone's arm. You will begin to notice that what you focus on expands. Document the evidence of your item throughout the week here:

_____

_____

_____

_____

_____

DAY 50 Date_____

MORNING PRACTICE

_____
_____
_____

AFTERNOON PRACTICE

_____
_____
_____
_____
_____
_____

EVENING PRACTICE

_____
_____
_____
_____
_____
_____
_____
_____

DAY 51

Date_____

MORNING PRACTICE

_____
_____
_____

AFTERNOON PRACTICE

_____
_____
_____
_____
_____

EVENING PRACTICE

_____
_____
_____
_____
_____
_____
_____
_____

DAY 52 Date_____

MORNING PRACTICE

_____
_____
_____

AFTERNOON PRACTICE

_____
_____
_____
_____
_____
_____

EVENING PRACTICE

_____
_____
_____
_____
_____
_____
_____
_____

DAY 53　Date_____

MORNING PRACTICE

_____

_____

_____

AFTERNOON PRACTICE

_____

_____

_____

_____

_____

_____

EVENING PRACTICE

_____

_____

_____

_____

_____

_____

_____

_____

_____

DAY 54 Date_____

MORNING PRACTICE

_____
_____
_____

AFTERNOON PRACTICE

_____
_____
_____
_____
_____
_____

EVENING PRACTICE

_____
_____
_____
_____
_____
_____
_____
_____

DAY 55 Date_____

MORNING PRACTICE

_____
_____
_____

AFTERNOON PRACTICE

_____
_____
_____
_____
_____

EVENING PRACTICE

_____
_____
_____
_____
_____
_____
_____

DAY 56 Date_____

MORNING PRACTICE

_____

_____

_____

AFTERNOON PRACTICE

_____

_____

_____

_____

_____

_____

EVENING PRACTICE

_____

_____

_____

_____

_____

_____

_____

_____

WEEKLY CHECK-IN

"Do not wait. The time will never be 'just right.'"
—NAPOLEON HILL

What is one realization or aha moment you had this week? How will it impact you going into next week?

_____

_____

_____

_____

_____

CREATE YOUR HAPPY

The real reason we want to manifest physical items, experiences, or people in our lives is because we ultimately believe that by having it, we'll feel happiness, joy, and excitement (some elevated state of being that we aren't currently experiencing). This mindset places us in a perpetual state of wanting and waiting for something to make us happy. The truth is that we create our happiness. Happiness is a choice, and it can be yours in every single moment. I invite you this week to look for a reason to be happy *in the moment*. It may be a trip to your favorite coffee shop, a long drive down a country road, a phone call with a friend, or even just a walk in the sunshine. Do what makes you happy, and you'll open up the floodgates for more reasons to be happy to manifest.

What Are You Waiting For?

The manifestation that you're calling in has a feeling associated with it that is truly what you're looking for. This exercise will help you identify what *feeling* you are waiting to feel. When you have clarity around the feeling, you can begin to create more of that in your life. In doing so, you will be on the same frequency to attract your manifestation, because like vibration attracts like vibration.

Choose one manifestation goal that you are working on. It can be a relationship goal, career goal, financial goal, or any other.

Next, complete this sentence:

When I have/achieve/earn _____, then I will feel _____.

Example: When I have my dream partner, then I will feel loved.

This *feeling* represents what you ultimately believe is lacking in your life. You don't need to wait for anything or anyone to come into your life to feel this feeling. You can begin to feel it now, in this moment.

MONTHLY CHECK-IN

*"What you get by achieving your goals
is not as important as what you become
by achieving your goals."*
—ZIG ZIGLAR

Take a moment to reflect on this month. What have been your greatest accomplishments so far?

_____

_____

_____

_____

_____

_____

Have any manifestations come to fruition? If not, does your desire still feel aligned?

_____

_____

_____

_____

_____

_____

CONTINUED ON NEXT PAGE

Embodiment is the key to magnetic attraction. This has been referred to as "fake it till you make it," but I prefer to reframe the concept to "be it until you see it." Here's why: In order to be able to fully realize your ideal reality, you first have to walk the walk and talk the talk. One of the best ways to be able to embody the version of yourself that is already living in the manifestation is to read real-life stories of people who have created/achieved the goal that you are pursuing. I recommend reading biographies of people who have achieved similar goals or following people who inspire you on social media. Imagine you are living this life by stepping into their reality. Feel what it feels like to have achieved this goal. I like to refer to these as "expanders" because seeing that other people have been able to manifest what you desire triggers mirror neurons in your brain and allows your subconscious to get on board with it also being possible for you.

It's Already Done

Somewhere in the realm of infinite possibilities, the desire you have has already manifested. There is a reality that exists right now, in this moment, where you are currently living in your ideal reality with all the magical manifestation in tow. This exercise will help you tap into that reality now and guide you toward being able to more fully embody that version of yourself.

Step 1: Close your eyes and imagine that you are stepping onto an elevator. Take the elevator up to the eleventh floor, and as the door opens, you notice a flight of stairs in front of you. Take the flight of stairs up to the big, beautiful door that awaits you. Knock on the door. As the door opens, you come face-to-face with yourself—the you that is currently living the reality of your dreams.

Step 2: As this version of yourself invites you in, take note of how it feels to be in your own energy. What does the environment look like? Are there plants, large windows, anything that stands out?

What are you wearing in this reality?

_____

_____

_____

Where do you live? Who do you live with?

_____

_____

_____

What are your daily habits?

_____

_____

_____

What beliefs does this version of yourself hold?

_____

_____

_____

Step 3: Embody this version of yourself *now*. Based on the information you received in this visualization, notice the ways in which you can begin to emulate this version of you. This could look like changing up your space to be more reflective of your ideal self. It could also be as simple as adjusting a belief system or adopting a new habit.

DAY 57   Date_____

MORNING PRACTICE

_____

_____

_____

AFTERNOON PRACTICE

_____

_____

_____

_____

_____

_____

EVENING PRACTICE

_____

_____

_____

_____

_____

_____

_____

_____

_____

DAY 58   Date_____

MORNING PRACTICE

_____
_____
_____

AFTERNOON PRACTICE

_____
_____
_____
_____
_____
_____

EVENING PRACTICE

_____
_____
_____
_____
_____
_____
_____
_____
_____

DAY 59 Date_____

MORNING PRACTICE

_____

_____

_____

AFTERNOON PRACTICE

_____

_____

_____

_____

_____

_____

EVENING PRACTICE

_____

_____

_____

_____

_____

_____

_____

_____

DAY 60 Date_____

MORNING PRACTICE

_____
_____
_____

AFTERNOON PRACTICE

_____
_____
_____
_____
_____

EVENING PRACTICE

_____
_____
_____
_____
_____
_____
_____
_____

DAY 61 Date_____

MORNING PRACTICE

_____

_____

_____

AFTERNOON PRACTICE

_____

_____

_____

_____

_____

_____

EVENING PRACTICE

_____

_____

_____

_____

_____

_____

_____

_____

DAY 62 Date_____

MORNING PRACTICE

_____

_____

_____

AFTERNOON PRACTICE

_____

_____

_____

_____

_____

_____

EVENING PRACTICE

_____

_____

_____

_____

_____

_____

_____

_____

DAY 63 Date_____

MORNING PRACTICE

_____

_____

_____

AFTERNOON PRACTICE

_____

_____

_____

_____

_____

_____

EVENING PRACTICE

_____

_____

_____

_____

_____

_____

_____

_____

_____

WEEKLY CHECK-IN

"Always give without remembering and always receive without forgetting."

—BRIAN TRACY

How did you show up for yourself this week? Going into next week, what can you do to support yourself more?

_____

_____

_____

_____

_____

_____

GIVE WHAT YOU WANT TO RECEIVE

The fastest way to teach the universe that you have faith in your ability to generate abundance is to freely give. What we give freely affirms the belief that we already have it. When you demonstrate this through the act of giving, you are opening yourself up to being able to receive even more. If you want more appreciation, give someone a compliment. If you want more money, increase the size of the tips that you leave. Whatever you want more of in your life, practice giving it away this week. This practice is truly an embodiment of your belief in the infinite supply of the universe, and as you give, so you will receive.

The Vacuum Method

The universe works like a vacuum in the sense that it fills unoccupied space. This can work in your favor or to your detriment. In order to allow for the new to enter, we have to make space for it. Clinging to the old will only delay the arrival of what we're calling in. If we aren't willing to make the space, the universe will often step in and clear the path for us. When you take the initiative first, it tends to be a gentler experience. This exercise will help you identify the areas of your life that could use a little spring cleaning.

Take a moment to reflect on the manifestation you're calling in. If it were to come right now, in this moment, would you be fully prepared to receive it?

Meaning . . . would you have the space for it? For example, if you're calling in a new relationship but your old relationship is still lingering, you may need to let go of this old energy so the new can enter.

How can you begin to make space in your life now for what you're asking for?

Examples:

Manifestation: a new, leveled-up wardrobe

Space to clear: empty the closet, donate old clothes

Manifestation: a trip to Bali

Space to clear: block off time in your calendar for your "trip to Bali" and tell your friends about it!

Your turn:

Manifestation: _____

Space to clear: _____

DAY 64 Date_____

MORNING PRACTICE

_____
_____
_____

AFTERNOON PRACTICE

_____
_____
_____
_____
_____
_____

EVENING PRACTICE

_____
_____
_____
_____
_____
_____
_____
_____
_____

DAY 65   Date_____

MORNING PRACTICE

_____

_____

_____

AFTERNOON PRACTICE

_____

_____

_____

_____

_____

_____

EVENING PRACTICE

_____

_____

_____

_____

_____

_____

_____

_____

_____

DAY 66 Date_____

MORNING PRACTICE

_____

_____

_____

AFTERNOON PRACTICE

_____

_____

_____

_____

_____

_____

EVENING PRACTICE

_____

_____

_____

_____

_____

_____

_____

_____

DAY 67   Date_____

MORNING PRACTICE

_____

_____

_____

AFTERNOON PRACTICE

_____

_____

_____

_____

_____

_____

EVENING PRACTICE

_____

_____

_____

_____

_____

_____

_____

_____

_____

DAY 68 Date_____

MORNING PRACTICE

_____

_____

_____

AFTERNOON PRACTICE

_____

_____

_____

_____

_____

EVENING PRACTICE

_____

_____

_____

_____

_____

_____

_____

_____

DAY 69

Date_____

MORNING PRACTICE

_____

_____

_____

AFTERNOON PRACTICE

_____

_____

_____

_____

_____

_____

EVENING PRACTICE

_____

_____

_____

_____

_____

_____

_____

_____

DAY 70

Date_____

MORNING PRACTICE

_____
_____
_____

AFTERNOON PRACTICE

_____
_____
_____
_____
_____
_____

EVENING PRACTICE

_____
_____
_____
_____
_____
_____
_____
_____
_____

WEEKLY CHECK-IN

> *"Our intention is everything. Nothing happens*
> *on this planet without it."*
> **—JIM CARREY**

What is one lesson you learned this week? How can you apply it
going into next week?

_____

_____

_____

_____

_____

LIVING INTENTIONALLY

Most of our lives are spent on autopilot, moving from task
to task without being intentional about our actions. Becom-
ing a conscious creator means tuning in to yourself moment
by moment and directing your point of focus. Creating small
intentions and acting on them is one of the fastest and most
influential ways to train your subconscious mind. Practice being
intentional throughout your day with mundane little tasks. Say
to yourself, "I am going to go to the bedroom and make the bed"
and then follow through. Not only does this help you live more
purposefully but it always builds trust. When you say you're
going to do something and follow through with it, this sends
a strong message to your subconscious that your word holds
weight. Confidence is a by-product of self-trust.

Align Beliefs with Intentions

As discussed, our beliefs are the driving force behind what we are able to create and allow in our lives. When the subconscious mind believes something to be true for you, it will look for reasons to validate and create it in your reality. In order to reinforce a belief, we have to essentially convince ourselves that it's true. This exercise will help you align your intentions with your beliefs.

Step 1: Choose an intention or a goal that you're focusing on at the moment.

My intention is to _____.

Example: My intention is to attract more financial stability.

Step 2: Create three statements that would be useful for you to believe in order for this to be true.

Example: Money is an unlimited resource that easily flows to me whenever I need it.

_____

_____

_____

_____

_____

_____

CONTINUED ON NEXT PAGE

Step 3: Integrate the new statement into the subconscious mind using the physical body. The body is a representation of the subconscious mind, and what we *feel* to be true is what we translate into belief.

Repeat to yourself something that you already know to be true.

Example: My name is _____ and I am _____ years old.

Repeat this several times and feel the level of certainty in your body as you make this statement.

Next, repeat the new belief with the same tone and physicality as you stated the above. Hold your body in the same way and repeat it with the same level of certainty. Repeat this process throughout the day. It takes practice, but over time it will start to feel "true," and this is an indication that it's rooted in your subconscious.

DAY 71 Date_____

MORNING PRACTICE

_____

_____

_____

AFTERNOON PRACTICE

_____

_____

_____

_____

_____

_____

EVENING PRACTICE

_____

_____

_____

_____

_____

_____

_____

_____

DAY 72 Date_____

MORNING PRACTICE

_____

_____

_____

AFTERNOON PRACTICE

_____

_____

_____

_____

_____

AFTERNOON PRACTICE

_____

_____

_____

_____

_____

_____

_____

_____

DAY 73 Date_____

MORNING PRACTICE

_____
_____
_____

AFTERNOON PRACTICE

_____
_____
_____
_____
_____
_____

EVENING PRACTICE

_____
_____
_____
_____
_____
_____
_____
_____
_____

DAY 74 Date_____

MORNING PRACTICE

_____

_____

_____

AFTERNOON PRACTICE

_____

_____

_____

_____

_____

_____

EVENING PRACTICE

_____

_____

_____

_____

_____

_____

_____

_____

DAY 75 Date_____

MORNING PRACTICE

_____

_____

_____

AFTERNOON PRACTICE

_____

_____

_____

_____

_____

_____

EVENING PRACTICE

_____

_____

_____

_____

_____

_____

_____

_____

DAY 76 Date_____

MORNING PRACTICE

_____
_____
_____

AFTERNOON PRACTICE

_____
_____
_____
_____
_____
_____

EVENING PRACTICE

_____
_____
_____
_____
_____
_____
_____
_____

 **Date**_____

MORNING PRACTICE

_____

_____

_____

AFTERNOON PRACTICE

_____

_____

_____

_____

_____

_____

EVENING PRACTICE

_____

_____

_____

_____

_____

_____

_____

_____

_____

WEEKLY CHECK-IN

"Passion is energy. Feel the power that comes from focusing on what excites you."
—OPRAH WINFREY

What manifested for you this week that you want more of? Less of?

_____

_____

_____

_____

_____

FOLLOW YOUR EXCITEMENT

The secret to finding your purpose lies in moments of passion and excitement. What you feel excitement about or what you can concentrate on without effort is a clear indication of the path toward your purpose. I believe that we don't find our purpose—our purpose is always there in the form of passion that simply needs to be remembered. Following what excites you the most in every moment of the day will act like little stepping-stones to take you down the path of abundance.

Close your eyes and imagine that you are walking down a beautiful path in nature. In the distance, you can see a golden light. As you proceed toward the light, you notice that there is a gold chest on the path. You make your way toward the chest and place your hands on it. You can feel your excitement and anticipation about what's inside.

As you open the chest, you notice the surge of energy moving through your body. Take note of what you see inside. You may see symbols, items from childhood, pictures, etc. Allow the energy of this chest to ignite a passion within you.

Tap into Your True Passion

As we get older, many of us lose sight of our true passion. Somewhere along the line we decide that it's either silly, not realistic, or even "embarrassing." If our passions aren't accepted by our parents or society, we will likely ignore them and replace our passion with something more practical. This exercise is designed to help you get back in touch with your soul's calling.

What are some things that you loved to do as a child?

_____

_____

_____

_____

_____

_____

_____

_____

_____

_____

CONTINUED ON NEXT PAGE

What are you doing when it seems as though time passes
unusually quickly?

_____

_____

_____

_____

_____

_____

_____

_____

What would you be doing if money wasn't an issue?

_____

_____

_____

_____

_____

_____

_____

_____

_____

What would you be pursuing if you wouldn't be labeled or judged negatively for it?

_____

_____

_____

_____

_____

_____

_____

_____

_____

_____

This exercise should give you some clarity around what your soul is calling you toward. Remember: Abundance follows passion. Decide to add more of what you truly love to your life and watch how doors begin to open, because the universe always supports you in the pursuit of what excites you the most.

DAY 78 Date_____

MORNING PRACTICE

_____

_____

_____

AFTERNOON PRACTICE

_____

_____

_____

_____

_____

_____

EVENING PRACTICE

_____

_____

_____

_____

_____

_____

_____

_____

DAY 79 Date_____

MORNING PRACTICE

_____

_____

_____

AFTERNOON PRACTICE

_____

_____

_____

_____

_____

_____

EVENING PRACTICE

_____

_____

_____

_____

_____

_____

_____

_____

DAY 80 Date_____

MORNING PRACTICE

_____
_____
_____

AFTERNOON PRACTICE

_____
_____
_____
_____
_____
_____

EVENING PRACTICE

_____
_____
_____
_____
_____
_____
_____
_____

DAY 81   Date_____

MORNING PRACTICE

_____

_____

_____

AFTERNOON PRACTICE

_____

_____

_____

_____

_____

_____

EVENING PRACTICE

_____

_____

_____

_____

_____

_____

_____

_____

_____

DAY 82 Date_____

MORNING PRACTICE

_____
_____
_____

AFTERNOON PRACTICE

_____
_____
_____
_____
_____
_____

EVENING PRACTICE

_____
_____
_____
_____
_____
_____
_____
_____
_____

DAY 83 Date_____

MORNING PRACTICE

_____
_____
_____

AFTERNOON PRACTICE

_____
_____
_____
_____
_____
_____

EVENING PRACTICE

_____
_____
_____
_____
_____
_____
_____
_____

DAY 84   Date_____

MORNING PRACTICE

_____

_____

_____

AFTERNOON PRACTICE

_____

_____

_____

_____

_____

_____

EVENING PRACTICE

_____

_____

_____

_____

_____

_____

_____

_____

WEEKLY CHECK-IN

"The moment of surrender is not when life is over. It's when it begins."

—MARIANNE WILLIAMSON

What, if any, patterns or cycles repeated for you this week? If none, what would you have to believe is true to experience this?

_____

_____

_____

_____

SURRENDER AND LET GO

One of the most difficult parts of the manifestation journey is surrendering control and letting go of the way we think things should unfold. Surrender is often seen as a sort of "giving up." However, surrendering is not about giving up on our dreams or our visions; it's about trusting that we don't need to manifest the path . . . we just need to follow it as it unfolds. When we surrender to the universe, we begin to go with the natural flow and let go of the resistance. This actually speeds up the process of letting in what you desire. You can tell where you're holding on too tight to things when you get caught up in the "how." For example, how is this all going to work out? The moment you notice yourself in the "how" of it, you are trying to create the path. Here is a quick meditation to help you release the "how" to the universe.

CONTINUED ON NEXT PAGE

Close your eyes and imagine that you are in a room filled with bright light. There is a table in this room with a box on top of it. Make your way over to the box. Next to the box, you notice a piece of paper with a pen. Take a moment to write down everything that you are trying to control, predict, or cling to right now. When you feel your list is complete, go ahead and open the box. Inside you can see a golden energy swirling around (similar to a ball of light). Place the piece of paper inside the box, allowing the golden energy to take the paper into it. Place your hands over your heart and say in your mind or out loud, "I release you and surrender my worries to the universe. I trust the unfolding of the path for my highest good and the highest good of all. Thank you."

Releasing Resistance and Doubt

It's absolutely normal to experience resistance and doubt along the manifestation journey. Resistance is a sign that you are stepping into uncharted territory. This is a good thing because it means you're stretching yourself outside your comfort zone. Anytime you step to the plate and say, "I want more and I'm choosing to grow," you will be faced with all the old limiting thoughts that liked you better where you were. The mind will always seek to keep you safe, but it's not always working in your favor.

This exercise will help you reflect on ways you may be allowing doubt to stop you.

Step 1: What manifestation have you been working toward that hasn't yet manifested or that you feel resistance around?

_____

Step 2: Fill in the blank:

_This _____ can't happen for me because_

_____

_____

_____

Whatever comes to mind during this self-inquiry is the seed of doubt that is creating a block around your manifestation.

Example: This relationship can't happen for me because who is going to want to be with someone my age?

The doubt: My age has implications for my ability to find a loving partner.

Step 3: To release your doubt, it's time to find evidence to discredit this belief. Surely you can find someone who has accomplished what you desire, or you can even see evidence in your own life where this proved not to be true.

What evidence do you have to discredit this doubt?

_____

_____

_____

MONTHLY CHECK-IN

*"Follow your heart, stay aligned with
your source of being—love—and let the
universe take care of the details."*

—WAYNE DYER

What has been the biggest takeaway for you this month? What have
you been able to manifest so far?

_____

_____

_____

_____

_____

WHEN IT'S NOT HAPPENING

Sometimes we can do all the right things, check all the boxes,
and still not see the glimpse of hope that what we want is on
the way to us. Here's the thing: Just because it hasn't happened
doesn't mean it's not coming. The secret is to remain consistent
with the process and to not give up. Think of manifestation like
going to the gym: You have to stay consistent in order to have
consistent results. I recommend making manifestation part of
your morning routine.

Grab a drink, take out a journal and pen, and light a candle
to set the tone. Start with a few things you're grateful for, really
feeling that gratitude. Notice how you're feeling and any thoughts
that surface. Then set a few manifestations for each day. What

would you like to accomplish or manifest? Spend a few moments visualizing completing each of your manifestations and allow yourself to feel it as if it's done. Set it and let it go!

What's Next?

Now that you have a pretty solid foundation of the manifestation process as a whole, you know how important it is to have a target or a set point for what's next. This exercise will help you unleash your deepest desires and start setting the mark for your next chapter.

Step 1: Think of something you'd like to manifest next. Maybe it's something you're still working on or something entirely new.

_____

_____

_____

_____

Step 2: The "why"—why do you want this?

_____

_____

_____

_____

What feeling do you think having this will bring you?

_____

_____

_____

CONTINUED ON NEXT PAGE

Step 3: Get specific! Describe your manifestation in great detail. If it's a partner, list everything you would like in a partner (I mean *everything*). The more specifics you add, the easier it is for your subconscious and the universe to make it happen.

_____

_____

_____

_____

Step 4: What do you need to believe is true in order to allow this into your life?

_____

_____

_____

_____

Step 5: Create an affirmation that enforces the new belief.

_____

_____

_____

_____

Tip: Use the 369 method to reprogram your mind with the new thought!

A Final Note

Congratulations on completing *369 Manifestation Journal for Beginners*. I want to take a moment to celebrate you for taking this bold step toward changing your life. It's not always easy to take that step and to be open to new ideas, but you did it and you should be proud of yourself (regardless of what has or hasn't manifested).

My hope is that this work has opened you up to a whole new set of possibilities and has inspired you to keep going, to keep dreaming big. Now that you have the tools you need to be an intentional creator, stay focused on where you want to go and allow manifestation to become a lifestyle so you can live life to the fullest. You are truly only one decision or one mindset shift away from an entirely different life.

Don't ever forget that you have the power within you to be and have anything that you desire. Your power always lies within, and you are worthy of it all.

I wish you all the best on your journey ahead!

Resources

BOOKS

Ask and It Is Given: Learning to Manifest Your Desires by Esther and Jerry Hicks

Change Your Thoughts, Change Your Life: Living the Wisdom of the Tao by Dr. Wayne W. Dyer

The Reality Creation Technique by Frederik E. Dodson

The Secret by Rhonda Byrne

Super Attractor: Methods for Manifesting a Life Beyond Your Wildest Dreams by Gabrielle Bernstein

PODCASTS

Expanded Podcast by To Be Magnetic™

The MANIFEST by Sarah Prout

You Can Have It All by Lindsay Rose

References

Angelou, Maya. *The Heart of a Woman*. New York: Random House Publishing Group, 1981.

Brown, John F. *The Gift of Depression: Twenty-One Inspirational Stories Sharing Experience, Strength, and Hope*. Koloa, HI: Inspire Hope Publishing, 2001.

Byrne, Rhonda. *The Secret*. New York: Atria, 2006.

Carrey, Jim. "Jim Carrey on the Power of Intention." Accessed June 6, 2022. youtube.com/watch?v=8qSTHPABoHc.

Dyer, Wayne W. *I Can See Clearly Now*. Carlsbad, CA: Hay House, 2014.

Ferraro, Kris. *Manifesting: The Practical, Simple Guide to Creating the Life You Want*. New York: St. Martin's Essentials, 2021.

Fraga, Kaleena. "Inside Nikola Tesla's 3, 6, 9 Obsession and the Unusual Theories It Spawned." Accessed June 6, 2022. allthatsinteresting.com/nikola-tesla-3-6-9.

Hicks, Esther, and Jerry Hicks. *Ask and It Is Given: Learning to Manifest Your Desires*. New York: Hay House, 2004.

Hill, Napoleon. *Napoleon Hill's Positive Action Plan: 365 Meditations for Making Each Day a Success*. New York: Penguin, 2009.

_____. *Think and Grow Rich! The Original Version, Restored and Revised*. Anderson, SC: Mindpower Press, 2015.

Nightingale, Earl. *The Strangest Secret*. Shippensburg, PA: Sound Wisdom, 2019.

"Nikola Tesla Quotes." Accessed June 6, 2022. goodreads.com/author /quotes/278.Nikola_Tesla.

Shinohara, Ryuu. *The Magic of Manifesting: 15 Advanced Techniques to Attract Your Best Life, Even If You Think It's Impossible Now (Law of Attraction)*. Independent, 2019.

Williamson, Marianne. *A Return to Love: Reflections on the Principles of a Course in Miracles*. New York: HarperCollins, 1992.

Ziglar, Zig. *Inspiration from the Top: A Collection of My Favorite Quotes*. Edinburgh: Thomas Nelson, 2012.

Acknowledgments

I want to thank each and every person who has crossed my path through this journey we call life. Without you, I wouldn't have become the woman I am today. I want to thank my mom, Rose Herczeg, for being my number one fan. And to my friends and clients far and wide . . . thank you for believing in me and loving me through it all. Your unwavering support has given me the opportunity to do what I love, and for that I am eternally grateful.

About the Author

 Lindsay Rose is a manifestation coach and expert on quantum creation. Manifestation has truly changed her entire life, and she now teaches people all over the world how to create the life of their dreams. Her passion is to educate people on the truth about how manifestation works, giving them a solid foundation of quantum physics, neuroscience, and practical application of a self-developed formula for magnetic attraction. She lives her life as an example to others that you can have whatever you desire and is the embodiment of what she teaches.

CPSIA information can be obtained
at www.ICGtesting.com
Printed in the USA
JSHW040042200723
45076JS00009B/160